THIS BOOK
BELONG TO

_____

_____

_____

TEST YOUR COLORS HERE

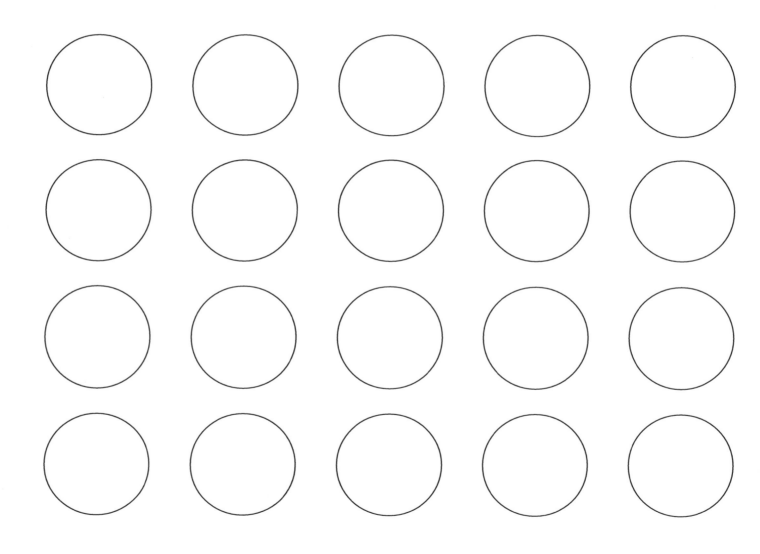

Freedom
isn't free.

Bravery endures time.

Gratitude in
every salute.

Remembering our defenders.

Land of liberty, thanks to veterans.

Courage, sacrifice, honor.

Made in the USA
Las Vegas, NV
08 November 2024

11388127R00024